MAKING SIBLING TEAMS WORK:

THE NEXT GENERATION

Craig E. Aronoff, Ph.D.
Joseph H. Astrachan, Ph.D.
Drew S. Mendoza
John L. Ward, Ph.D.

*Family Business
Leadership Series, No. 10*

Business Owner Resources
P.O. Box 4356
Marietta, Georgia 30061-4356

ISSN: 1071-5010
ISBN: 1-891652-00-1
© 1997
Second Printing

Family Business Leadership Series

We believe that family businesses are special, not only to the families that own and manage them but to our society and to the private enterprise system. Having worked and interacted with hundreds of family enterprises in the past twenty years, we offer the insights of that experience and the collected wisdom of the best and most successful family firms in North America.

This volume is a part of a series offering practical guidance for family businesses seeking to manage the special challenges and opportunities confronting them.

To order additional copies, contact:
Business Owner Resources
Post Office Box 4356
Marietta, Georgia 30061-4356
Tel: 1-800-551-0633

Quantity discounts are available.

Individual volume price: $14.95

Other volumes in the series include:

Family Business Succession: The Final Test of Greatness

Family Meetings: How to Build a Stronger Family and a Stronger Business

Another Kind of Hero: Preparing Successors For Leadership

How Families Work Together

Family Business Compensation

How to Choose & Use Advisors: Getting the Best Professional Family Business Advice

Financing Transitions: Managing Capital and Liquidity in the Family Business

Family Business Governance: Maximizing Family and Business Potential

Preparing Your Family Business For Strategic Change

Developing Family Business Policies: Your Guide to the Futur

CONTENTS

EXHIBITS

I. Introduction: The Crucial Generation

Welcome to the world of sibling partnerships. When it is the best of all possible worlds, brothers and sisters harmoniously and successfully run their family business for another generation and their family serves as a center of strength, joy, love, and support.

In your dreams, you say? For some families, these goals sound impossible. Yet, we have seen many sibling groups perform beautifully as teams, and we have also seen the transformation of dysfunctional, disharmonious sibling groups into high-performing partnerships. Our experience has shown us that teamwork consists of a set of skills and attitudes that can be learned, and this book is aimed at helping the siblings in your family business become an effective, cohesive, fully functioning partnership.

We have found that it takes the effort of three groups to assure that siblings can evolve into teams and work together successfully:

- Parents
- In-laws
- The siblings themselves

If you are a parent, meaning you are probably the founder of your business, **you have the opportunity to position your children for success as a sibling team**. Your role is not an easy one. Mastering it is somewhat like mastering the rhythm and intricacies of a dance. This book will help you understand the dance and, we hope, enable you to execute the steps with skill and grace.

If you are the husband or wife of a second-generation family business member, your role is tricky indeed. You may be both loved and in some ways feared by your spouse's family. We explain why and show how you and the members of the business-owning family can work toward a more harmonious, trusting relationship—one that not only supports your marriage but also supports the sibling team of which your spouse is a part.

If you are now or expect to become part of a sibling team running a family business, you have a more challenging role to fill than you ever dreamed of. How you and your siblings handle this responsibility is more than crucial. Not only do you have the responsibility of preserving the business, you must also make it grow significantly so that it can support your families and your children's families (and not just one family, as it did in your parents' generation). You must

1

make a success of the business in your own generation and set the stage for the generation that follows you. What you do as a sibling team and how you do it will serve as the model for your children and will have consequences—good or bad—not only in their generation but in generations yet to come.

This is a very vulnerable time in the life of your family business. Most family firms don't make it to a third generation. However, we are dedicated to the proposition that you and your siblings can pilot your business and your family through this critical phase, and this book is designed to help you do just that. It is full of wisdom, tips, guidelines, and the experiences learned from other families. Nevertheless, we encourage you to "think outside the box." Our suggestions and ideas are meant to stimulate your own thinking. We call attention to the issues you must think about and talk about, point to the many tough decisions you will have to make, and offer suggestions for building and maintaining a smoothly operating sibling team. But ultimately, your challenge is to design creative solutions that best fit your family business and your family's situation.

What you do as a sibling team and how you do it will serve as the model for your children and will have consequences—good or bad—not only in their generation but in generations yet to come.

Just as a given problem has more than one solution, a number of different sibling arrangements work. Here are four of them:

- **The "all in, all owners" team,** in which siblings are employed in the business and all are owners. They interact frequently and function largely as co-equals. Although they may have different positions, each has a say in major decisions.

- **The siblings "in the business" team,** composed of only those siblings who work in the business. Every quarter or so, they meet with their other siblings who are not in the business. Those in the business interact regularly and hold frequent meetings.

- **The sibling ownership team** consists of owner/siblings both inside and outside the business. While those in the business meet regularly to focus on operational issues, the ownership team meets periodically to discuss ownership issues.

2

- **The sibling board team** occurs when all siblings comprise the membership of the board of directors.

These teams may overlap and, in the course of a generation, configurations may change—a sibling may leave the business, another may want to join, and still another may want to sell his or her stock. Teams are fluid, and the wise family will maintain flexibility.

This book is written primarily for sisters and brothers who work in their family's business and/or are very active owners—that is, they are involved, informed, and interested in the business, or want to get that way. They care.

Also keep in mind our bias: our goal is to retain the integrity of the family while serving the business. We believe that a strong, healthy family enhances the possibility for a strong, healthy business, and vice versa.

II. *The Era of Sibling Partnerships*

This could be called the Age of Sibling Partnerships. Where once a business was almost invariably handed down from a father to a son, we are seeing a major shift in which businesses increasingly are passed from a founder to a next-generation team of siblings.

The immediate future will see enormous changes in the leadership of family businesses in the United States. According to the recent *American Family Business Survey*, a massive study that we conducted in conjunction with Arthur Andersen and MassMutual, 28 percent of the family firms polled expected their CEO to retire within five years, and an additional 14 percent said their current CEO would semi-retire within the same period. The study showed that **11 percent of family businesses now have co-CEOs and an amazing 42 percent are considering moving to co-CEOs in the next generation.** Many factors drive this trend:

> *Where once a business was almost invariably handed down from a father to a son, we are seeing a major shift in which businesses increasingly are passed from a founder to a next-generation team of siblings.*

- **Parents are increasingly inclined to welcome all their children into the business.** First-born sons are no longer presumptive successors. The tendency of many parents is to treat all children as equals. In the business families that we work with, we are called upon less and less to help work out problems between an entrepreneurial father and a successor son and more and more to help families in the development of a next-generation team as managers and/or owners.

- **Women are seeking more active roles in the management of their families' businesses and are more likely to be considered for top positions.** In the *American Family Business Survey*, more than 40 percent of the families considering co-CEOs in the next generation said that one of those co-CEOs may be a woman. Finding daughters assuming leadership positions in what have been, until now, male-dominated industries is no longer unusual.

5

- **Young people are demonstrating more enthusiasm for the family business than ever before and, in our observation, are returning to the family firm in greater numbers.** Perhaps one of the reasons for their enthusiasm is the seemingly growing trend toward appreciation for the family.

- **Ever accelerating change means that the knowledge of younger people is more valuable to their family businesses.** Wisdom that was applicable in the past is less likely to be applicable now or in the future. Founders recognize the contribution that their sons and daughters can make in keeping a business on the cutting edge.

- **The laws that currently govern estate transfers support the formation of sibling teams.** Gifting stock rather than cash has tax advantages, and if you gift stock to all your children, then suddenly they've become business partners.

- **Greater awareness that many successful sibling partnerships exist makes others more willing to consider such partnerships.**

Perhaps your family is considering a sibling partnership for its business, or perhaps brothers and sisters have already begun the difficult but rewarding process of developing themselves into a team of leaders. Even if the prospect of a sibling team seems off in the distant future, you will see, as you read on, that farsightedness now will pay off for your business and your family should such a team come into being. It is not too early to start thinking about the possibility.

III. What Makes The Sibling Generation Different

Each generation of a family business is unique and faces its own special set of challenges. We believe, however, that the sibling team—frequently the second generation—faces some of the most difficult challenges of all. **If you are a member of a sibling group, be prepared to spend enormous effort to building and maintaining an effective team. The demands on your time and energy will be exceptional, and you will have to work very hard.** However, the rewards will be great. What could be better than a harmonious, extended family, able to enjoy the financial returns of a prosperous business and able to pass that business along to a well-prepared next generation?

We generally find the sibling partnership stage to be more intense and volatile than any other. As a result of their growing up together, the level of intimacy and emotionality is higher among siblings than, for example, the cousin generation that follows. And because siblings carry into the business all those memories and opinions of each other that they have held since childhood, the possibility for harmful misunderstandings is strong.

Unlike cousins, siblings have probably grown up in a business founded by their parents. They tend to be very emotionally connected to the business, to their parents, and to each other. Hence, the intensity.

What also sets the siblings apart and can lead to volatility is that there are fewer of them than there are cousins at the cousin stage. Because each sibling may own a substantial minority position in the company, a family business can be threatened when one sibling is angry, disenchanted or unproductive, and isn't functioning as part of the team. Buying that person's shares can wreck the capital structure or the strategic plans of the business.

Another characteristic of the sibling stage is that Mom and/or Dad are probably still alive, and they have an enormous influence on the team and on the business. They will exert forces that the siblings must learn to recognize, understand, be compassionate about, and cope with as a unit. Further, the siblings must develop the ability to communicate effectively and sensitively—again as a unit—with their parents about business and family issues.

On the plus side, their intimacy and shared experiences provide siblings in a family business with great motivation to live with and

7

benefit from their differences.

Nevertheless, the differences can be profound and it is crucial that brothers and sisters in a family business learn to tolerate and resolve them. Otherwise, **differences and misunderstandings can become "historical" ones, painfully passed down through future generations.**

Four Tasks

To assure the continued success of the business and the family, sibling partnerships have four distinct and vital tasks:

1. **Become an autonomous independent team.** This means independent of Mom and Dad. And while parents will talk about how much they want this to happen, unconsciously they may not want it to happen and may not let it happen. The tug-of-war in which the sibling group tests its autonomy and the parents assert their power is almost as natural as night and day.

2. **Take the initiative as successors.** You can't just wait until the business is handed to you. Too often, the sibling generation waits for the parents to make the first move. The more the sibling generation takes responsibility for and control of developing themselves individually, developing themselves as a team, and seizing the initiative, the more likely it is that succession is going to happen in a timely and successful way. Yes, occasionally a patriarch will see sibling interaction as a plot or conspiracy to get rid of him, but that doesn't happen often. So, while taking the initiative may be somewhat risky, our experience suggests that the benefits outweigh the risks.

3. **Put structure and strategies into place that will help the business grow significantly.** You have grown up in a family that probably had a good standard of living. But the business needed to support only one set of parents and children. Now, each of you wants your own family to live at least as well as your parents and their family did. For that to happen, the business has to grow sufficiently to support all siblings and their families.

4. **Position the next generation for success.** The job is not done until the stage is properly set for handing off the business to your own children. This means putting into place policies, procedures, and structure that will support the success of the next generation of family business owners and leaders. A generation of cousins may

not be able to do its job until the generation just before it finishes its job.

Emotional Issues

A number of factors unique to brothers and sisters will deeply affect how you work together as a team. We regard them as major emotional issues. Understanding them and realizing that every sibling partnership is affected by all or most of these issues will help you be more objective, more knowledgeable, and even more compassionate about dealing with them. Your increased awareness will truly empower you as a group. Let's explore what the emotional issues are:

☞ **The controlling behavior of entrepreneurial parents.** Many entrepreneurs are "high controllers." Combining an entrepreneur's tendency toward control with normal parental feelings can produce parents who want to govern the attitudes, the values, the opinions, the dress—in short, the behavior—of offspring, not just while they are children but throughout life. The business itself can feed the need to control. For example, a business-owning family can be highly visible in the community, giving parents concern about how the things their children do might reflect on the business.

☞ **The effect of parents' behavior on the development of children's skills for success.** While they usually don't mean to, parents may adopt behavior that precludes the development of the siblings as a team. For example, instead of providing opportunities to learn the skills of shared decision-making, parents may make all decisions themselves. Instead of helping the next generation learn to resolve conflict, they may suppress conflict. Instead of encouraging the development of communication skills within this next generation, they create a system in which each parent communicates individually with each child. Instead of allowing learning from failures, they try to protect their children from mistakes. That creates massive pressures on members of the next generation not to fail.

☞ **Sibling rivalry.** As adults trying to work as a unit in business, members of the next generation need to see each other in new ways—even learning to know each other all over again. As individuals, **each sibling may consciously have to strive for less dependence on parental approval to minimize the rivalry felt toward brothers and sisters.** This situation can be remedied by siblings'

9

approval becoming more important than parents' approval.

☛ **"Adopting" your parent's "baby."** (How hard it is for them to give it up!) It is often said that a business is the parents' "other child." They created it, just as they created their human children, and their feelings for it are profound, just as their feelings for their real children are profound.

☛ **The age spread of the siblings.** Those who are older are the first to enter the business and get a "running start." An individual with a running start gains tremendous advantages in a situation where the family is trying to develop an equal team. And, because they love their children equally, the parents may champion and support the underdog—the younger sibling, who hasn't had a chance yet or who hasn't had as much time in the business.

If the age spread is, say, eight years, at one end of the spectrum you have a 34-year-old who feels ready to begin leading the business and at the other end, a 26-year-old who is just getting started. At the same time, the family is already at a stage where decisions must be made about leadership succession, who gets the voting stock, and other major issues. It is important to look at how the difference in ages affects the team and to find ways to compensate for various perspectives, levels of maturity, and extent of experience or knowledge.

☛ **Mother's tendency to want to "save the family."** Often, a mother's desire to preserve the family is so strong that she may become involved to the point of manipulating or moderating any news that she picks up about disagreements or disputes in the business. Siblings need to be aware that this is a common pattern and to address it sensitively.

☛ **The "in-law effect."** In the second generation, for the first time, "outsiders," in the form of spouses, are introduced into the family and, by extension, into the family business. Unless care is taken, all sorts of negative emotions can surface: fear, mistrust, suspicion, envy. But, as you will see later in this booklet, with the commitment of siblings and parents, the in-law effect is manageable.

☛ **The challenge of diversity within the sibling group.** Even though siblings have the same parents and grew up in the same house, each is likely to be very different, with different views and abilities. Sally may be visual; Sam, verbal. Esther may be extroverted; Herb, analytical.

Differences should be valued because they strengthen a team and can produce better decisions. But, because differences can also create friction, they may be a weakness. Siblings need to acknowledge that they hear, think, decide, and communicate differently. They also need to develop skills to deal with their differences—communications skills, listening skills, empathy, and appreciation for differences. Sometimes it may help to remember the United States' motto: *e pluribus unum*—out of many, one.

EXHIBIT 1 ▬▬▬▬▬▬▬▬▬▬▬▬▬▬▬▬▬▬▬▬▬▬▬

Goals for Sibling Teams

- Take charge of succession. Stop waiting for your parents' permission.
- Overcome sibling rivalry.
- Demonstrate your ability to work together.
- Convince parents that there won't be a bloodbath once they leave the business. (Otherwise, they won't leave.)
- Communicate with your parents and with nonfamily executives as a unit.
- Communicate openly with one another.
- Develop a code of conduct.
- Become an autonomous, independent unit.
- Put structures and strategies in place that will help the business grow significantly in your generation.
- Position the next generation for success.

By understanding these emotional issues, members of the sibling group become better prepared to compensate for weaknesses and build on the strengths that will help them accomplish the four tasks set forth at the beginning of this chapter: Becoming an independent team; taking the initiative as successors; putting structures and strategies in place to make the business grow; and positioning the next generation for success.

IV. *The Farsighted Founder*

For a business founder, it is never too early to begin thinking about and planning for the transition of the business to the next-generation sibling team. In fact, how children are treated even when they are small and how they are reared can help that future partnership be successful. All that's needed is incredible foresight and the willingness to resist some of one's own basic instincts!

If you are the family business' founder, think for a moment about your personality and the way you run your business. As a founder, you may find that you are hard-driving, and given to making your own decisions and making them fast. Those traits may work well in the founding generation. Founders need those characteristics to work through and survive all the difficulties and challenges of starting a business and to resist the naysayers who insist it can't be done.

But your business will likely require a different type of leadership in the second generation. If your children are to function effectively as co-owners and/or fellow employees, they must adopt procedures and practices far different from the ones that were successful for you. What works for the lone, aggressive, entrepreneurial founder will *not* work at the sibling stage.

*What works for the lone, aggressive, entrepreneurial founder will **not** work at the sibling stage.*

We see four major tasks for the parents/founders, and all of these tasks require thinking ahead to the time when the business is in your children's hands. These tasks include:

☛ Rearing your children in ways that encourage and set the stage for their working together as an independent unit.

☛ Adopting personal behavior—toward each other as a couple, toward your children, and toward their spouses—that supports a sibling partnership.

☛ Putting policies and practices into place that will provide a foundation for the partnership, and encouraging the sibling team's efforts to continue that process.

☛ Preparing for your exit from the business.

Let's take these one by one:

Preparing the kids: Many founders worry greatly that the kids won't get along together when they grow up. If they can't get along together now, how will they own or run a business together in the future? When children are very young, and as they grow older and become teenagers and young adults, much can be done to nourish their ability to work together and to channel sibling rivalry into constructive pursuits.

We recommend to parents that they act as though their business will evolve into a sibling partnership at some point in the future. At the very least, this means avoiding telling an oldest child, "This business will be all yours someday." That statement may come back to haunt you as the other children grow up and demonstrate more business ability or interest than the oldest child.

To prepare them for a future partnership, brothers and sisters as early as their preteen years can be given tasks to do together that have consequences. For example, consider these assignments, which are appropriate for siblings from ages 8 to 18:

- Give them $100 as a group (or $1,000 or $10,000). Tell them you want them to figure out what stocks to invest the money in. Ask them to come up with a plan for learning about the stock market together and agreeing on what stocks to buy.

- Ask the kids to decide together by a specified date where the family will go on its next vacation. Tell them that if they can't agree, they won't get to go on vacation and Mom and Dad will go by themselves. The older they are, the more details they can decide.

It is a good idea to take the younger children aside individually and verify that they agreed with the decision—the oldest child shouldn't be allowed to dominate the decision.

In one family, the children were responsible for the business' float in their community's Fourth of July parade. In another family, which had a summer home on a lake, the children's love of water skiing became the focal point of team building at an early age. They had to take turns, with one sibling skiing, another operating the boat, and still another spotting the skier. They had to learn to cooperate with one another, to look after each other's safety and welfare, and to manage the cost of fuel for the boat and keep the boat in good repair.

When you give children tasks of this nature, you help them build skills for success as a team: communications, conflict resolution,

14

EXHIBIT 2 ■■■■■■■■■■■■■■■■■■■■■■■■■■■■■■■■■

Ten Tips for Founders

1. Assume that your business may evolve into a sibling partnership. Avoid saying to any one of your children, "Someday this business will be all yours."

2. From the time your children are young, promote the partnership skills of listening, communicating, resolving conflict, and working together.

3. Recognize that what works in the founder's stage of the business often will not work at the sibling stage. Your children have to re-invent the company.

4. Before they're needed, put policies and procedures in place that will support the sibling partnership.

5. Introduce the concept of prenuptial agreements early—before the kids have serious boyfriends and girlfriends.

6. Welcome in-laws and educate them about the business.

7. Treat the sibling team as a unit. Don't try to divide and conquer.

8. Let leadership among the siblings emerge.

9. Practice patience. Don't always step in when things aren't going smoothly.

10. Plan your retirement, and implement the plan.

---

and shared decision making. It is hard to do, but parents need to resist the temptation to step in with a solution. When parents step in, the children are deprived of the opportunity to work things out themselves, as a unit. We recommend, instead, an "oversight" approach—letting the kids work things out with parents refereeing only enough to make sure that nobody really gets hurt.

The same strategy can be used when the children grow up and begin working together in the business. Give your children meaningful tasks that have serious consequences and force them to come up with solutions. You may think it is a high-risk strategy, but in our experience, it almost always works.

When the children are in their 30s, we advise parents to tell them to create the succession plan. The directive might go something like this: "Come up with a succession plan. When you all agree with it 100 percent, bring it to us. Unless we see something that's terribly wrong, we'll agree with it and let it go forward." The challenge is in the siblings' hands, and they have to figure out a way of getting over their rivalries or using their rivalries to advantage so as not lose their ability to be a part of the business.

Keep throwing tasks at your children that they must accomplish as a unit. Some parents separate their children, giving each independent responsibilities, hoping to avoid conflict and confrontation among them. Indeed, having independent responsibilities is critically important, too. But what *makes* a team is giving the siblings a job to do *together* so that they can develop their working relationships. What breaks the team is depriving them of the opportunity to work things out together.

Parents can also expose their children to other leadership models. Encourage them, in teams of two or more perhaps, to visit successful businesses where leadership is structured differently and to share with the family what they learned. Invite representatives from other family businesses that have team leadership in place to your family meetings to talk about how their system works—and what works well and what doesn't.

Personal Behavior

Entrepreneurs' actions provide powerful examples and valuable lessons, creating a model for the next generation. Every couple, for example, has disagreements. It is helpful to acknowledge differences as a couple and not let your disagreement get lived out through the children. For example, in some families where the parents are in discord, one child may affiliate with the father and another with the mother. In this way, discord among the children is born. Make clear to the younger generation that the parents' problems as a couple are the parents' problems, not the children's; make clear, also, that the siblings' problems as siblings are their problems, and they must learn to deal with them.

Parents also need to avoid "triangulation" at any age. Say all the siblings are now in the business and Mark, the youngest, is consistently late for work. Mom expresses her displeasure not to Mark but to his sister, Susan. In this instance, Mom should talk to Mark about his tardiness and leave Susan out of it. (And when parents triangulate, we advise their offspring not to permit it. Susan, in this case, could say, "Mom, that's something you should take up with Mark.")

Entrepreneurs' actions provide powerful examples and valuable lessons, creating a model for the next generation.

Parents have a natural inclination to develop individual relationships with each of their kids. Doing so can be fun and enriching for parent and child. In a family business, however, where you're trying to support the development of a sibling partnership, such relationships, if not managed carefully, can sabotage team development by enhancing communications skills between parents and children, rather than between siblings. It may also inadvertently encourage siblings to strengthen ties with Mom or Dad rather than with each other. The trick for parents is to find a balance: concentrate on treating the siblings as a unit, to help them develop partnership skills; enjoy individual relationships with each when appropriate—that is, when doing so doesn't undermine the team-building process.

Another area where parents must monitor their own behavior is in their treatment of their children's spouses. In-laws are so critical to the success of a sibling partnership that we have devoted a whole section to the topic (see page 21). Parents can do much to set the tone for acceptance of in-laws as partners, welcome them into the family, and acculturate them into the business.

Giving conscious thought as a family to the role of spouses in the family business is a good thing. When parents and siblings can reach a consensus about the in-laws' role, the involvement of in-laws becomes a matter of policy rather than personalities—in other words, spouses aren't excluded just because someone in the family doesn't like George's wife.

Policies and Practices

If you've been an especially farsighted founder, you already have an outside board in place—that is, a board with independent business peers on it in addition to key family members. You may also have begun to establish some formal policies for the business—such as a code of conduct for the family or guidelines for the employment of family members.

Parents go a long way toward setting up their children for success when they, as founders, begin to establish procedures and practices that will serve the next generation well. **By initiating family meetings in the first generation of a family business, for example, you set a precedent for open communication and mutual decision making.** When Maria becomes the CEO in your children's generation, she will already have learned the value of communicating with her brothers and sisters and sharing business information with them. She will also have a model for doing so.

If you are like most founders, however, you have neither a board of directors nor written policies. The next generation must establish the practices and policies that will enable the business to grow, thrive, and survive to the third generation. Keep in mind that whenever the members of the next generation develop a policy or establish a procedure, they are gaining strength and experience in working as a team. Remember, too, that in seeking family and business growth, they need to transform an entrepreneurial, informal organization to one governed and managed by more formalized, institutionalized policies, procedures, and systems. Also recognize that the second generation is working to prepare the family and the business for a third generation of leadership, sustaining the entrepreneur's legacy.

Exit Planning

No business owner's job is done until she or he has planned to exit. This means not only planning for family and business leadership succession, but also providing for financial transitions in the family business through appropriate estate planning. According to a study conducted by Kennesaw State University, 86 percent of U.S. family business owners surveyed said they had done estate planning beyond a basic will. But 70 percent of all surveyed could not estimate their estate-tax liabilities, and 43 percent could not estimate their business' market value.

Planning your exit from a business—and sticking to the plan— is much more an emotional issue than it is one of money. Most business owners love their work and many don't want to let go. They haven't considered what they would do in retirement.

Upon becoming CEO in his middle 50s, one son who had experienced years of brutal power struggles with his father turned to his board and announced that he would retire at age 62. He told the members of the next generation to figure out the next transition and get ready—he would help and provide resources in the form of consultants. "If my dad had said that to me at any time," he said, "that would have been the greatest thing he could have done for me." In effect, this CEO told the next generation: "It is my job to make this your job."

The Ideal

Ideally, what will happen is this: The parents will follow the practices and suggestions outlined above, encouraging and developing the team-building skills of their children, first when they are very young and later as they are young adults in the business.

At the most advanced level of the succession stage—when the children are in their 30s (though some may yet be in their 20s) and before or during the time when the ultimate leadership model for the business is chosen—the parents delegate the leadership of the business to a "sibling executive committee." In effect, **the parents and the partnership of siblings develop a joint venture or co-venture that will last over a period of time.** The parents say to the siblings: "You are now, collectively, the chief operating officer of the company." The parent-CEO remains the chief executive, in charge of strategic decisions.

This process allows the parents to see how well the siblings work together. It also reveals how much they *want* to work together—which may ultimately decide for them whether they are in fact going to be a sibling partnership over the long term. The process also enables the sibling team to begin to develop their own leadership and decision-making systems.

What the process requires of parents is patience. The key is that parents *not* step in and take command when things aren't going smoothly—when, for example, differences surface among siblings and the executive team becomes paralyzed, decisions get made slowly or not at all, or a poor decision is made. The parents have to be willing to accept some negative business consequences as a cost of learning and going forward.

Another reason a founding parent may need patience is that the indecision and the time the team process takes may be viewed

The parents have to be willing to accept some negative business consequences as a cost of learning and going forward.

19

as signs of weakness. **Entrepreneurs pride themselves on being decisive and reporting to nobody. The process of the sibling team goes against the grain.** (An outside board can be invaluable here, coaching the siblings to make better decisions, for example, or helping them to manage conflict and use it constructively.)

Over time, several years perhaps, the solution to future leadership emerges from the team. With the help of the board, the siblings begin to see for themselves who can really lead the business.

An alternative to this ideal occurs when it becomes extremely apparent to the parents that there is one proper leader and they decide—sooner rather than later, when Bill is 32, not when he's 52—that he is on the path to becoming the next CEO. Such a decision may be made because Bill is so clearly able, or because he is able and ready but his siblings are still very young and their abilities still have not emerged. The parents find themselves in a position of having to make a choice, and they do so lovingly, expressing their appreciation for the other children and including them as part of the ownership team. The process of transition to Bill as CEO may take five years or more to complete. Meanwhile, his siblings have an opportunity to adapt and accommodate to the decision and to decide whether or not they wish to commit themselves to the company with Bill at the helm, or get another job, or go to graduate school and move on with their lives.

Even when Bill becomes CEO, he cannot simply play the role his parents played. The relationship among siblings is much different from that of parents and children. It takes much more time, effort, and communication to maintain sibling support than to gain children's acquiescence.

V. In-Laws or Outlaws?
Making Siblings' Spouses a Part
of the Team

When Angela married David, she was excited about joining a high-energy, well-respected, affluent family in a small, midwestern town. True, she had to move from her beloved California, and leave behind a teaching job. But David was excited about joining the manufacturing firm his grandfather had started and working in partnership with his sister and two brothers, and Angela was sure she could find a teaching job in her new community. Angela admits she became a little unnerved when, shortly before the wedding, David's parents insisted that she and David sign a prenuptial agreement that prevented her from receiving any assets of the business if she and David ever divorced. It hurt her feelings to think that the family didn't trust her, but David seemed just as hurt and angry as she was, so she signed and the wedding proceeded.

What Angela didn't expect was the isolation she felt once she and David were settled in their new home. She felt like a foreigner—instead of making her feel welcome, David's family seemed to regard her with suspicion. What's more, David complained that his father treated him unfairly, and when Angela lovingly sided with him, his sister and brothers began to treat her coolly. To top it off, David worked such long hours that it seemed like he had no time for Angela. Just when Angela was thinking she had made a big mistake marrying David and wondering if she should return to California, she discovered she was pregnant.

Angela's experience is a composite of the many stories we hear from in-laws. It is extremely difficult to be an in-law in a family business. And, in the sibling generation, in-laws—"foreigners" who have grown up in a different culture—are introduced into the business for the first time.

The presence of in-laws makes a business-owning family edgy. And not without reason. According to our Arthur Andersen/MassMutual *American Family Business Survey*, 22 percent of family businesses report that at least one family member has gone through a divorce in the last five years.

Frequently, in-laws may be regarded as culprits. In fact, however, more often the siblings themselves and, secondarily, their parents, are the real culprits. If the in-laws become a negative

force in a family business, it is often a result of the behavior or neglect of the siblings and parents.

The danger for family businesses is that an unhappy, angry spouse can threaten a sibling partnership and destroy any sense of team. In addition, unless the business is protected by prenuptial or shareholders agreements, an embittered spouse can gain access to assets and cripple a family company financially.

Problems also occur when in-laws promote and defend their spouses or battle for status and rewards. An in-law may complain to family members that his wife is underpaid and underappreciated. One spouse may be upset because her brother-in-law has a more exalted title than her husband, or be jealous over the fact that someone else in the family has a bigger house or fancier car. Or, in family meetings, in-laws may offer non-business perspectives on business issues.

A happy spouse, on the other hand, can support a sibling partnership and contribute to its strength.

Some in-laws call themselves "outlaws"—they feel they are that remote from the family's business. Parents, however, cross their fingers and hold their breath when their children get married. They worry that unpredictable and uncontrollable additions to the family might disrupt the already challenging task of running the business.

But we urge families to view the situation from the perspective of the in-law. With empathy, understanding, acceptance and education, families can help spouses support the family business and the sibling partnership.

In-laws often experience culture shock when they enter their new families. Unless they come from a business-owning family, they have little understanding of what to expect. As one new daughter-in-law put it: "The family business is the central topic every time family members get together. If you aren't closely involved in the business, you feel left out."

> *"The family business is the central topic every time family members get together. If you aren't closely involved in the business, you feel left out."*

Sometimes in-laws can feel overwhelmed by the energy and enthusiasm of the tightly knit families into which they have married. Or they may feel in a bind: If they don't ask enough questions about the business, the family thinks they lack interest; if they ask too many

22

questions, they are regarded as nosey. They'd like to know more but hesitate asking basic questions for fear of seeming naive or stupid. When they side with a husband or wife in conflict with a parent or sibling—as any good spouse would do—they incur the wrath of the family.

What often leads to these problems is that the in-law—let's say a daughter-in-law—learns most of what she knows about the family from her husband. David, for example, comes home from work and complains to Angela that his father isn't paying him enough, especially compared to his brother, Steve, who doesn't work very hard and frequently takes off from work to play golf. Or he worries that his father won't approve of a decision he made that day. Angela begins to develop resentment toward her father-in-law and Steve. Unwittingly, David has begun to poison the relationships between Angela and his father and brother. What's more, Angela begins to worry that David isn't as strong and independent as she once thought he was.

What needs to happen instead is that business-owning families should immediately begin to acculturate new in-laws, helping them to feel like valued members of the team. Siblings, parents, and in-laws can take conscious steps that lead to a sense of membership for in-laws and avoid spoiling relationships with the family.

What Siblings Can Do:

- As part of your code of conduct (See page 34), make a pact that you will champion and support one another to your spouses. Promise not to complain about each other to your spouses. Agree that your sibling relationships are precious to you and inviolable and will not be compromised by your marriage relationships (and vice versa!).

- If you have a problem with one of your siblings, do all you can to settle it before you go home. Don't take it home with you.

- As a team and as individuals, work to develop independence from the need for parental approval.

- If relationships are reasonably healthy, include spouses in meetings of the sibling generation, even if you're talking mostly about business issues. This helps build their support for the unity of the sibling team. It also gives them the opportunity to get information firsthand.

- Develop individual relationships with in-laws. Then, if problems arise, deal with the in-law directly, one-on-one.

What Parents Can Do:

- Pave the way for in-laws to become part of the team. Spend time educating them about the family's business. Explain business finances and the requirements for business success. Involve in-laws in regular family meetings, and encourage lots of basic questions.

- Be empathetic. Allow for mistakes and confusion. If you are the wife of the business owner, for example, invite your new daughter-in-law to lunch and talk to her about how you were once in the same position, and how you learned about the family business.

- Play up the strengths of your children's spouses. We know a daughter-in-law who is a musician. Her husband's family makes it a point to attend her performances and to talk with her about her career. Such recognition not only helps in-laws develop self-esteem in their new family but also helps a business family broaden its own interests.

- Be open with information. Discuss issues such as compensation policies for family members.

- Ask new in-laws to describe their families' holiday and vacation traditions. Work to honor traditions on both sides. Be sensitive to siblings who choose to be with their in-laws on special occasions.

- Establish times when discussing the family business is off-limits.

- If prenuptials are required in your family, make clear that they apply to all family members and explain the reasons for their existence.

What Siblings' Spouses Can Do:

- Recognize that a sibling partnership is time-consuming and demanding. Being a part of such a team is one of the most difficult tasks your spouse could undertake. He or she will need your patience and understanding.

- Don't take sides or serve as an advocate for your spouse. If you think your husband or wife is being treated unfairly in the business, let your mate work it out.

- Learn all you can about your spouse's family business and about family businesses in general. Many colleges and universities

24

across the country have programs that family members can attend. Read the entire **Family Business Leadership Series,** and *The Family Business Advisor* newsletter. Magazines like *Family Business, Nation's Business,* and *Forbes* can also be helpful.

- Develop friendships with members of your spouse's family. This enables the family to know you as a person and helps build trust.

- During family business meetings, don't bring in nonbusiness perspectives on business issues. It is not appropriate, for example, to complain that your husband's boss does not appreciate how hard he works. Evaluating executives is the job of the business' management and board.

We can't emphasize enough that spouses be included in family meetings, and that the extended family find ways to have fun together—family retreats, family vacations, holiday and birthday celebrations and such.

When you include them in meetings, spouses begin to feel part of the system. They get messages and information that are not filtered through their husbands or wives, and they're able to form their own opinions about other family members independently of their spouses. They get to see their spouses in action, so they're not just depending on the "heroic" tales that the spouses tell about themselves.

When spouses are involved in events that are just for fun, family members and in-laws get to know one another better, see each other's different dimensions, and grow in appreciation of one another. And that supports the sibling team.

A Quick Word About Prenuptial Agreements

For many families who own businesses, prenuptials are a good idea. But be aware of these caveats:

(1) As far as the business-owning family is concerned, **the primary purpose of a prenuptial agreement should be to preserve the ownership of the business within the family. From the family business standpoint, a prenuptial agreement should focus on ownership of stock in the family business and related assets.** Any issues to be addressed other than stock should be left up to the couples themselves.

25

(2) **Plan ahead. Start thinking and talking about prenuptial agreements before any child has a serious relationship.** Thinking about prenuptials after an engagement can create bitterness. Thinking about prenuptials after marriage is usually too late. The best practice is for the family to agree prior to any siblings' engagement that prenuptial agreements will be the family's policy. The younger generation should understand why such agreements are necessary and be able to communicate that understanding to future potential spouses.

(3) **Require prenuptial agreements of all family members.** Don't require an agreement just because Jason is marrying a woman you don't like. By stipulating prenuptials across the board and explaining to future in-laws the reasons behind the family's policy, you stand a better chance of creating and maintaining in-laws' good will.

EXHIBIT 3 ▆▆▆▆▆▆▆▆▆▆▆▆▆▆▆▆▆▆▆

Premarital Agreements Are More Likely To Hold Up When. . .

■ **Full disclosure is made.** Each person should provide the other with a complete description of his or her finances, including assets and debt, and a statement of expected gifts, inheritances, and potential acquisitions and earnings.

■ **Each party is represented by his or her own attorney.** This helps assure that each party receives independent counsel and adequate financial disclosure prior to signing.

■ **The agreement is fair and "conscionable."** The wealthier party, for example, cannot cause the spouse to become a public charge by removing all support and other property rights.

■ **Both parties enter the agreement voluntarily.** Both must be of legal age and the signing must not be the result of coercion, duress, or undue influence.

■ **The contract is signed well in advance of the marriage.** Last-minute signing might be viewed as "under duress."

26

■ **Couples adequately define property as "separate" and "marital" or "community."** Separate property is that brought to the marriage or received by gift or inheritance during the marriage and, in the event of divorce, is not subject to being shared with a spouse. Marital or community property is that which is acquired during a marriage and is subject to an "equitable" division upon divorce.

VI. *Building A Healthy Team*

Turning any group of people into a team is a tough assignment. Forging two or more siblings into a team, especially if they didn't have team-building experiences growing up, is even tougher. The emotional issues we talked about earlier frequently get in the way—all the more reason to be aware of and understand these issues so that any negative impacts can be minimized or prevented altogether.

Consider two brothers, Evan and Arthur. Evan is 39, eight years older than Arthur. Evan views himself as highly responsible and sees Arthur as someone who is somewhat irresponsible and just living off the fat of the family business. Arthur, after all, was the baby of the family. For the first eight years of his life, Evan had been the center of attention and praise. Then Arthur came along and Evan had to fend for himself while little Arthur had everything taken care of for him.

To this day, Evan treats his younger brother like a baby and Arthur reacts like one. To make matters worse, their parents, seeing that they aren't working well together in the business, intervene and make decisions their sons should be making or hold onto responsibilities their sons should be assuming.

EXHIBIT 4 ■■■■■■■■■■■■■■■■■■■■■■■■■■■■■■■

Some Key Decisions Sibling Teams Must Make

- How shall we make decisions?
- What will our code of conduct be?
- What will our leadership model be? If a single CEO, who will that person be?
- How shall we accommodate the simultaneous goals of the family and the business?
- Who shall our advisors be? Who should be on our board of directors?
- How will we make this business grow? What should our strategy be?
- How will we communicate with our parents? With nonfamily executives?
- What policies will we put in place?

Working out the issue of family relationships makes team-building among siblings unique. And when parents haven't helped their children develop the skills for team success, the siblings, as adults, must develop those skills—including communications, conflict resolution, and shared decision making—on their own. What's more, as we stated earlier, for the sibling partnership to work, it must be autonomous from the parents. In addition, the siblings must find a healthy balance between relating as a unit to their parents and, when appropriate, relating to them individually.

Among the issues that Evan and Arthur will have to work out is their age spread. If they are to succeed as partners, they need to let go of the roles in which they have become stuck: as big brother and baby brother. When they can shed these long-held views of each other, the more ready they will be to learn to treat each other as equal, responsible adults, capable of running a business together. If their parents continue to intervene, they must find a way, as a unit, to take on more responsibility and not let their teamwork be compromised by Mom and Dad.

As a group of siblings who are committed to being a team but who may be beginning to work together in the family business for the first time, keep two things in mind:

Almost every group stumbles initially. Developing a team usually involves taking two steps forward and one step back. Don't lose heart in the early going.

Usually, groups go through four predictable stages popularly referred to as "forming, storming, norming, performing." The meaning of "forming" is obvious—a group of individuals come together for a specific purpose. They decide to become a team. At the beginning, however, they face "storming," meaning they experience conflict and disagreement as they try to get to know each other and the differences in their personalities and goals surface. Especially at this stage, there may be heated arguments, protection of turf, and occasionally tears. Remember, this is a tough stage. But you'll find yourselves getting through it and reaching the "norming" stage, when you get used to each other, rules are agreed on, and you find ways to work together effectively. And finally, you reach the desired stage, "performing," when, during the best of times, you are functioning together like parts of a smoothly running, well-oiled machine.

Expect conflict, and regard differences as an asset. Conflict is a given. Even though you come from the same family, each sibling is an individual, very different from any other. Those differences are an asset because they bring a variety of talents, perspectives, and ideas to the table. **With the commitment of everyone on the team and with the right structures, systems and procedures in place, conflict can be managed effectively and your differences can be capitalized on for the benefit of the company and of the family.**

Developing Critical Skills

While the spirit of wanting to work as a team is essential, agreeing to be a team is not enough. Critical skills must be developed and the members of the group must share an attitude that supports the notion of partnership.

The key to partnership is the ability to focus on something larger than yourself—the good of the business or the family, for example, or the mission of the family or the business. Having a larger goal enables many a family to work through conflicts and rivalries and get beyond self-interest and ego.

Finding common ground is another important key. When families having difficulties focus primarily on their areas of conflict, they may find their problems intractable. Members jump in and say, "Let's start hammering these out." And they achieve little progress and much frustration, unless they are skillful enough to get beneath the surface and uncover underlying issues. However, doing that requires a high level of self-confidence on everyone's part. It may call for the help of an outside professional.

Families that seek common ground take the time to understand why they're together doing what they do, celebrating and appreciating that first, and building their commitment to it so that conflicts won't tear them apart. Then they give recognition to their areas of differences and say, "Let's work on those."

A sibling team can begin the same way. In fact, the members of each new generation of owner-managers should, at the beginning of their partnership, spend some time discussing why they are in this business together and asking such questions as, "What does this business mean to me?" "Do we want this business to continue for our grandchildren, and if so, what steps do we need to take to position our company for the future?" And saying "grandchildren" here is important because it helps remove the question from the vested interest that each sibling might have in his or her own children.

EXHIBIT 5 ███████████████████████████████

How To Bring About Creative Solutions

Resolving conflicts requires patience and skill. Here are some steps that siblings will find useful:

- Define the problem first; don't start by presenting a solution.

- Prove you understand the other person's concerns by restating them and asking if that understanding is correct.

- Put all your energy into debating the **issue.** Don't allow yourself to get personal. We believe in the saying: "Attack the problem; support the person."

- If resolution comes slowly, brainstorm more alternatives. Ask others to propose new alternatives without initially evaluating any of them.

- If the going gets tough, take a break. Come back to the topic the next day. In the meantime, resist dumping it on anyone else.

- Remember that how you address the problem will long be remembered. Think about what you say and how you say it. One family we know pretends that the discussion is being videotaped for next-generation viewing.

Once you've answered these questions and recommitted yourselves to the family business, and as you move forward as a partnership, you need to develop some critical attitudes and skills. Your team will grow in effectiveness when you, as individual members, grow in your ability to:

- Respect others and demonstrate that respect.

- Know yourself and the boundaries between yourself and others.

- Clarify your own feelings and take responsibility for them. As one member of a team said when he was disappointed with the way a particular decision went, "It is not everybody's job to cater to how I feel and make me feel better. It is my job to deal with my own feelings."

- Understand everybody's goals and help find solutions for attaining them.

- Accept and tolerate each other's differences. Try hard not to be judgmental of each other, whether it be over matters of taste, lifestyle, or choice of spouse.

- Empathize, but don't assume you already know others' views. Learn to listen to each other's perspectives.

It helps to think of yourselves as one family. As one business owner put it, he and his brothers agree to agree. They feel that unity is more important in the long run than any particular decision.

Two of the most stubborn issues sibling teams have to work through, as the story of Evan and Arthur illustrates, are sibling rivalry and the "baggage" that brothers and sisters bring to the workplace as a result of having grown up together. The development of communications tools like family meetings can help team members acknowledge and appreciate the overlap of family and business and develop a vision for the business.

By discussing their differences as a sibling group, brothers and sisters learn to cope with sibling rivalry and channel it in ways that benefit the business. Instead of saying, "Why aren't you more like me?," the group can assess their differences, explore what strengths those differences bring to the team, and see how they complement each other. The sibling team can say, "All right, we are different people. We're as different as night and day. It is as if we didn't even come from the same family. But we have a business to run. Let's articulate how we are different, accept those differences, and then creatively look for ways to capitalize on those differences to really help the family and the business."

Taking the attitude that your sister is an idiot and should change her way of seeing the world so she's more like you doesn't work. It is not, "Fix my brother," or "Fix my sister." The trick is not to look for ways to show the other person why he is wrong but rather for the team members to enter into dialogue that recognizes and respects each person's individuality.

Essential to learning to communicate with each other is breaking through the misinterpretations and misunderstandings that grow out of the past, when the siblings were children. As children, we adopt roles in the family. If Josh was a tease when he was 10 years old, his brother and sister may still regard him as a tease when he's

35, and, thinking they know him, they are likely to misinterpret what

EXHIBIT 6 ■■■■■■■■■■■■■■■■■■■■■■■■■■■■■■

Sample Family Code of Conduct

We believe in these principles as we share together in the vision we seek:

- We realize that what is good for the company is good for the family as a whole.

- We will all follow company rules (i.e., dress, timeliness, expense accounts, etc.)

- We will cherish our reputation for honesty and integrity.

- We will do all we can to promote and develop strong family loyalty.

- We recognize differences will exist. We will discuss them directly and privately.

- We will always respect the opinions of others. We are committed to resolving our disagreements constructively.

- We will prepare ourselves for family meetings. We will develop agendas for them.

- At family meetings, we will encourage all to speak out.

- We will speak well of each other to all outsiders. We will not argue in public.

- We will promote each others' positive strengths among ourselves and with our spouses.

- We will keep shareholdings within the family and have marriage contracts.

- We will assume personal responsibility for effective estate planning and openly share our plans with others in the family.

- We will try to know each other's personal goals and look for opportunities to support them.

- We will seek ways to give back to the community.

---

he says today in light of what he was as a child. If he protests and says, "That's not what I meant," they may think he has a hidden agenda. Occasionally, a perceptive member of the team can recognize and surface such misunderstandings and help other group members get over them. More often, it takes the help of an outside professional, such as a family business consultant with strong insights into family dynamics or a psychologist versed in family and business systems, to enable a sibling group to break through such misunderstandings.

Making Decisions

Your first task as a team is to **decide how to decide**. Discuss the options that are available to you. It is critical to develop a process that has integrity and credibility, one about which everyone agrees, "This is a good, fair, appropriate process." If anyone questions the process, that's going to cause schisms within the team.

Siblings may decide that they will make decisions by consensus. They'll talk and talk and talk until everyone agrees. The advantage of that method is that everyone buys into the decision. A disadvantage is that it may take a longer time to make decisions.

As suggested for co-CEO groups on page 53, siblings can decide that, after thorough discussion of an issue, a simple majority vote is sufficient for some decisions while major decisions—such as implementing a new shareholders' agreement or selling off a division—require a super majority or unanimity. The group agrees ahead of time that if a vote doesn't go your way and you're not happy about it, you are still willing to go along with it because you are committed to the group. In any case, the group should present itself as unanimous to the family and the business.

Other groups may choose to have one person making all decisions or authority for decisions rotating among group members. Some partnerships use cumulative voting. For example, if the group is voting on three issues today, you each have three votes, and you can each use your votes however you want—one per issue, two on one issue, or all three on one issue.

As part of deciding how to decide, siblings need to agree on what they'll do when they reach an impasse. We find families using a variety of methods—sometimes ingenious ones—to break ties and end stalemates. For example, if you break the tie this time, then it is Aaron's turn the next time and Rebecca's the time after that, until the tie-breaking privilege has been rotated around the group.

In some cases, the sibling team will turn to a trusted outsider for an opinion or mediation. We would discourage the sibling group from turning to their parents or the board as a tie-breaker, however. That puts them in the position of taking sides and, in the long run, can diminish their effectiveness.

Ultimately, the decision-making process is a reflection of how well the relationships in the group are established. When decision-making functions at its highest level, it is virtually invisible. It means discussions are going on behind the scenes. Group members are checking with one another, gauging each other correctly and interpreting each other properly. When the decision is put into place, everyone accepts it.

The Sibling Code

The process of developing policies provides a great team-building experience. Perhaps most important and the one a sibling team should agree on first is a code of conduct.

The code of conduct addresses such issues as:

- How are we going to treat each other?

- How are we going to make decisions?

- How and when do we communicate with each other?

- How will we handle conflict or disagreement?

- What do we say about each other to others—especially spouses and parents?

- How shall we manage our public image? Will Madeleine always speak to the media on behalf of the company or do we all get to share the limelight?

If your family does not already have a code of conduct, the one you produce may turn out to be a rich document that gathers some of the patina of old age over time and becomes part of your family tradition.

Strengthening Relationships

Building an effective team requires developing and maintaining good, trusting relationships with siblings. In time, for example, a take-charge leader will learn that she can't move ahead on her own when she has siblings as partners. Even though it takes longer, she will find that siblings need to be involved in the decision-making process in order to maintain their commitment to her as leader.

Developing the communication skills necessary for good team functioning takes practice. Learning to listen well and be sure you understand, learning not to let disagreement fester, learning to communicate directly, learning how to disagree without being disagreeable—all must be practiced until they become natural.

One way siblings support the team effort inside the business is to spend time together away from the business. Have fun together. Meet every week or two socially or on semi-business occasions, without spouses. This helps siblings to increase their interpersonal comfort with each other and enhance their interpersonal communications. The business should not be the only shared interest siblings have that keeps them together.

Continue your education

Shared educational experiences build unity. One way to create such experiences is to bring in a facilitator or family business consultant who can educate you on what a team is, how teams work, and the struggles that all teams face.

Education should be an explicit part of family meetings. Guest speakers, shared readings, and listening to or viewing audio- or videotapes on family business topics can be helpful. Some sibling teams attend university family business forums as a team.

Another way to learn is to visit other family businesses where sibling teams are operating successfully. One special advantage of such trips is the time the travelers spend together in a plane or a car, getting an opportunity to talk to each other and, on the way back, comparing what they heard and learned. An additional benefit is the opportunity to become revitalized and inspired when you see that sibling teams actually can succeed.

EXHIBIT 7 ▰▰▰▰▰▰▰▰▰▰▰▰▰▰▰▰▰

Pitfalls That Derail A Sibling Team

- Taking stands based on ego.

- Being unaware that someone — a nonfamily employee, perhaps — is playing team members off one another.

- Triangulation on the part of parents — that is, Dad complains to Karen about David but doesn't address David directly about the problem.

- Expectations that the leader should police the other siblings.

- Spouses who don't feel part of the team or welcome in the family.

VII. *Creating the Right Environment*

When leadership and ownership of a business move from the founder to next-generation siblings, the enterprise doesn't just change hands. It often moves from being an entrepreneurial, informally run business to one that needs more formal structures, systems, and procedures. This formalization is often referred to as "professionalization."

Done right, this institutionalization of what once might have been casual, intuitive processes will support the success of a sibling partnership and position the company for significant growth. It will provide a framework for decision making and planning as well as authority and accountability. It will set the standards for how the company operates and how the people within it conduct themselves. It will help the siblings recognize where business and family overlap and help them separate family issues from business issues. It will, in short, help the company move forward and prepare it for the cousin generation.

As much as possible, we strongly believe that systems should be in place before you need them. If it has not already done so, the sibling partnership now needs to be moving on such issues as how the family business will be governed, policies that should be developed, division of responsibility and authority, ownership and compensation structures, and communication in the business and in the family.

Governance at the sibling stage

Eventually, every family business needs a framework for making decisions and the orderly running of the company. In the most effective family firms, this often means a board of directors; a family council; and depending on the size and stage of the business, other decision-making or task groups; and a series of specific meetings that serve as basic tools of communication. Let's look at these elements as they pertain to a sibling partnership:

Board of Directors. Mom and Dad may have operated without a functioning board. Ideally, however, they would have a board with several respected independent outsiders on it or a less formal advisory council. If such a board does not already exist, in the sibling stage it becomes imperative. By "competent outsiders," we mean leaders from other well-run, successful companies.

A board becomes a forum that elevates discourse to the most constructive level. The independent outsiders can serve as a moderating force that can help the siblings resolve differences and encourage them to become independent of the parents. The outsiders also can mentor the siblings, encouraging them to form themselves into an effective ownership and/or management team.

An active board serves as an additional resource to the siblings, gives them feedback, and provides objectivity. The outside board members bring new and fresh information to the table. And they can prod the current generation to take the appropriate steps to prepare the next generation for leadership. They can assist in educating the siblings who are not active in the company and help them understand the realities of a business as well as their role in it.

The board provides incentive for the business' managers to discipline themselves and accept a certain level of accountability.

It also serves as a check and balance on siblings and parents alike. It can make sure the siblings aren't making unwise decisions. It can be a nudge that says, "Come on, you guys. If you're going to work together as a team, you've got to be more decisive than that." On the other hand, the board can also encourage Mom and Dad to be patient. Because the board is there, everyone behaves better. The board facilitates consensus, healing, and proactive behavior.

Meetings. In the sibling generation, the matter of meetings is somewhat simpler than it will become in the next generation when the family and business are larger. At the sibling stage, we see three types of meetings:

1. **Sibling team meetings**. These are meetings of the siblings who are active in the business. They meet regularly—possibly once a week—to review performance, plans and policies, and to keep each other informed. If all shareholders are active in the business, ownership meetings and sibling team meetings may be one and the same. If there are shareholder siblings who are not active in the business, then separate shareholder meetings two to four times a year may be instituted to build unity, communicate financial results, approve major transactions, or handle other matters restricted to ownership. (Meetings of family councils, which serve as the governing bodies of larger families, may be introduced in the next generation.)

2. **Family meetings**. These would include all siblings, spouses, perhaps older children, and parents. Held at least once a year, such

get-togethers provide the entire family with the opportunity to talk about such topics as the future, philanthropy, estate planning, family vacations, and the like. They are a great tool to make sure that there is appropriate and adequate flow of dialogue and information and communication among family members.

3. Board meetings. Held three or four times a year, these serve as a forum for strategic discussion, oversight, and accountability. The board represents shareholder interests and seeks to help management make the best possible decisions.

For a thorough discussion of governance, see Booklet No. 8 in the **Family Business Leadership Series**, *Family Business Governance: Maximizing Family and Business Potential.*

Policies

The beauty of policies is that they help a family business achieve success through the generations. Listen to the wisdom of one family-business owner: "I've learned that successful family businesses do a good job of anticipating future issues and talking about how to deal with them as a family *before* they become issues."

By developing policies, siblings are, in effect, agreeing on solutions to problems in advance. This helps prevent family members from taking issues personally and enables decisions to be more objective. In addition, sibling communication and problem-solving skills are strengthened.

Here are some of the policies that will benefit the family and the business at the sibling stage:

☛ **Code of Conduct**. Siblings agree on how they will treat one another and deal with conflict. For example, they can agree to support one another in public, to speak positively of one another to spouses, and to issue no ultimatums to one another. (For more on codes of conduct, see page 34 and Exhibit 6.)

☛ **Employment/Participation**. Families that emphasize that family members should prepare themselves through education and experience to make a real contribution to the business seem to find greater harmony and success. Many families also develop policies with regard to in-laws working in the business and to part-time employment. Policies governing qualifications for participation in the family business become increasingly important as the siblings' children become old enough to think about joining the business.

Some families also set standards for family members' participation on the board and for ownership in the business. To serve on the board of one family business, for example, a family member has to be of the caliber that some other unrelated company would select him or her for its board.

☞ **Compensation.** Open, explicit compensation arrangements are very helpful—they tell family members what they can expect and what is expected of them. Compensation policies also often address benefits, perks, and time off. (For more on this topic, see *Family Business Compensation*, No. 5 in the **Family Business Leadership Series**.)

☞ **Shareholders Agreements.** These are contracts among shareholders that specify rights and actions in respect to stock ownership under various circumstances, such as death, retirement, voluntary or involuntary separation from the business, divorce, or just the desire to sell one's shares. They enable a family to plan for stressful events. They may, for example, restrict who can be an owner of the business or may obligate a shareholder to sell shares when a triggering event occurs, such as retirement or disability.

☞ **Exit-Redemption.** Family members at any stage may need the freedom to opt out of a business strategy that the others have chosen. Likewise, they may need to be able to sell shares without guilt. That is, they should be able to let go of their shares without feeling that they are selling out or leaving their family. Financial mechanisms that provide liquidity to shareholders should be in place and they must be agreed upon in advance. One approach is to establish an annual shareholder redemption plan, a program that enables shareholders to sell stock to other shareholders or to the company within a set time period each year at a price established by formula or independent valuation. (For details, see No.7 in the **Family Business Leadership Series**, *Financing Transitions: Managing Capital and Liquidity in the Family Business.*)

☞ **Personal Investment Policy.** Siblings agree on how to handle new personal investment opportunities. If one, for example, learns of an attractive venture while talking to a customer or a supplier, does he or she share the information with other siblings?

If the business does not have a mission statement or the family does not have a family mission statement, the sibling team and other appropriate members of the family should set their development in motion. Other policies that siblings can put in place might govern:

- retirement age
- dividends
- company loans to family members
- ownership rights and responsibilities
- conflicts of interest
- ethics
- publicity
- how to assist family members in need.

Siblings will find it valuable periodically to revisit major issues like compensation, participation, corporate vision, and buy-sell agreements to see if the policies governing them continue to be appropriate and still have the group's support.

Compensation and ownership issues

Most experts advise families to pay family members according to market value—that is, what they would get for the same job in their industry if they worked outside of the family business. That's excellent advice, particularly for the third generation—the "cousin" stage—and generations beyond, when there are larger numbers of family members in the business and the business is larger.

It is also good advice for the years when siblings are entering the business and it is not yet clear that the business will develop into a sibling partnership.

Often, in the sibling generation, two or more siblings are actively involved in the business and hold top management positions. While their job responsibilities may vary slightly, the siblings may pay themselves equally when their positions and capabilities are approximately the same. Siblings who do so reason that the slight differences in job responsibility are insignificant relative to their equal ownership position, and see the attempt to discriminate among pay levels as not being worth the effort.

Siblings, whether they work inside the business or not, should understand the difference between compensation and distributions of profit. Compensation is pay (including perks and benefits) for

43

work performed in the business. Distributions are a reward for owners because they have put their capital at risk in the business. Owners who are not employed in the business may receive dividends. If dividends are paid, owners who also hold jobs in the business receive both compensation and dividends.

It is always important to keep shareholders not employed in the business involved as owners—keeping them informed, making them a part of family meetings, and inviting them to participate in appropriate decisions and committees.

We strongly recommend openness about compensation within the family. Salaries, benefits, and perks of family members in the business should be known to all adult shareholders. This diminishes the tendency of those outside the business to believe that those employed in it are earning far more than they actually are. (We also recommend a similar openness about estate planning. That is, estate planning—as it affects the business—should be coordinated among siblings.)

During the sibling partnership stage, siblings not working in the business should be treated as part of—and should feel part of— the ownership team. So what if one is a psychiatric nurse and another is a hockey player? Mom and Dad gave them equal shares in the business. They need to be involved, informed, and educated about their business. Their children may one day play an enormous role in the continuity and future success of the business.

EXHIBIT 8 ▰▰▰▰▰▰▰▰▰▰▰▰▰▰▰▰▰▰

Ways To Make Sibling Owners Not Employed In The Business Feel Included

- Communicate with them and educate them about the business.

- Invite them to family council meetings and family retreats.

- If qualified, ask them to sit on the board of directors.

- Make them part of the key ownership decisions—such as major strategic decisions, succession decisions, and major financial decisions.

- Seek a balance of power. One sibling may run the business, but a sibling outside the business may be in charge of family philanthropy.

- Include them and their families in all nonbusiness family gatherings.

- Adopt a "we're all in it together" attitude instead of thinking of yourselves as different branches of a family. Consider yourselves a tribe.

- Promote, support and champion nonactive siblings just as you do the active ones.

- Involve them in drafting policies to be ratified by the ownership— such as policies governing family members' employment or participation in the business.

- Invite them to oversee the writing of the family history.

Siblings and their parents will find it helpful to consider, discuss and determine what their "ownership vision" is. There are a number of ownership alternatives from which a family can choose. One is that there is a "first among equals," with the sibling who is CEO getting control. Still another is that siblings are treated differently—siblings in the business get more stock than siblings not in the business because the parents feel that it is important for the active children to have the controlling interest. Another possibility is to separate the value of the stock from the vote or control by issuing voting and non-voting stock. Each model can work, depending on the circumstances.

Choosing professional advisors and outside directors

As with the board of directors, the sibling partnership may need to develop its own set of professional advisors rather than "inherit" them from Mom and Dad. Just as there is a transition of leadership and ownership in the business, there may be a transition of advisors. Siblings who retain their parents' advisors sometimes find that those advisors reflect their parents' generation and are unsympathetic to the particular challenges of sibling partnerships.

In some instances, there may be a younger generation of advisors that can serve the sibling team well. For example, in the case of a good law firm, the 59-year-old senior partner who has always been Dad's lawyer may be wise enough to have a 33-year-old up-and-coming superstar begin to develop a relationship with the sibling team.

It is helpful for siblings to have one set of advisors, including outside board members, who serve them all as a group and who genuinely perceive their role as serving the ownership team more than serving the business. If an advisor sees himself or herself as serving the business, that advisor is likely to see the sibling who is CEO as the client. The CEO, after all, is giving the advisor work and approving the bills.

The sibling team should collectively choose the professional advisors and outside directors. They should represent or work with the group as a unit and see it as a team. Going along with a choice because he or she is one sibling's trusted friend or favorite accountant may cause a wedge in the group and threaten its unity. If any candidate seems more aligned to one of the siblings than to the others, move on to someone else. Every sibling should have a voice in and be happy with the choice, and every sibling should be satisfied that an advisor will see the whole team as the client. Each sibling, of course, can have his or her own advisor as well.

Nonfamily Employees

Professionalizing a family business means not only constructing the infrastructure described above but also putting into place the people who have skills that are best suited for larger organizations. This includes both family and nonfamily members.

As the sibling team begins to make the decisions and take the actions necessary to assure the success of a growing company, it needs to be sensitive to its relationship with the key nonfamily executives. The sibling team needs their collaboration. However, long-time, key nonfamily executives hired by the older generation may feel threatened by the processes of change from one generation to the next.

It is not unusual for nonfamily executives to assume that a political contest is going on among the siblings and to look to the parents for clues as to who the successor really is. The siblings may discover that nonfamily executives are playing one of them off another. Again, even if they are working in different cities, the siblings need to act as a unit in their relationships with nonfamily executives. The siblings need to get together and talk about how, for example, they're going to relate to the vice president of sales. "Do we offer encouragement? Is this a person we really want to promote in the future?" Through such discussion, the team can become united in its position and avoid sending mixed messages to the nonfamily executives.

In addition to being concerned about their own succession, some sibling teams take a broader view of succession that considers management development of nonfamily executives. They encourage their parents and board to understand where all the various executives fit, what their career plans are, and who the high-potential individuals in the company are.

The idea of having formal structures in a family business may seem strange at first for the family that hasn't had them. Families often prefer to think of themselves as being spontaneous and informal. But when a business is large enough to take the siblings in and will grow larger because of the contribution they make, it needs the order and framework for future growth that structure, policies, and procedures supply. It may take a while to learn to use these new tools effectively, but once you do, you will wonder how the business—and the family—ever did without them.

EXHIBIT 9 ▐███████████████████████████████████████

Pre-Conditions For Sibling Team Success

- **Redemption and exit plan.** A system that permits someone to exit and sell shares (including the pricing and terms) is in place. (Some families deliberately make exit impossible. If so, the arrangement should be legally binding and all should morally pledge to uphold it for the reasons it was chosen.)

- **An independent, outside board.** The best forum for debate and the best possible insurance policy, independent outsiders are a well-established part of the company's governing structure.

- **Siblings' code of conduct.** The team has explicitly agreed and committed to writing how it will make decisions, resolve conflict, treat each other, deal with the press and the public, conduct business affairs openly and ethically, and relate to each other.

- **Proven success at conflict resolution.** All team members trust that serious problems can be overcome without the intervention of parents.

- **Experience with open disclosure.** Each knows and accepts past and present salary and perks arrangements. All should know about any parental support and gifting.

- **Method of future compensation.** A process is in place to set future salaries, bonuses, and dividends, and to audit perks and financial relationship with the business and each other.

- **Completed, known estate plans.** These arrangements assure security to spouses and children and have been finalized and shared with each other.

- **Participation agreement.** All understand who can work in the business and who can own stock, including consideration for spouses, children, stepchildren, other relatives, etc.

- **Familiarity and comfort with outside directors and key advisors.** All members of the sibling team have good personal relationships with the directors, lawyers, accountants, and other important consultants.

- **Consensus on future of key nonfamily executives.** All respect the others who make the business successful.

- **Shared sense of purpose.** The duties and burdens of ownership are acceptable because business continuity has significant meaning for every team member.

VIII. *Choosing A Leader*

As we discussed in Chapter IV, we like to see the leadership solution evolve over time. When the siblings work together as an executive team, they begin to develop their own leadership and decision-making systems. And the choices available to the family become clearer.

Families can choose one of two basic models of leadership: (1) The more traditional model in which one son or daughter is singled out as the CEO, with siblings in other key roles; or (2) the increasingly popular "office of the CEO" arrangement, in which two or more members of the next generation share the CEO title. As mentioned in an earlier chapter, 11 percent of family firms now have co-CEOs and a startling 42 percent are considering moving to co-CEOs.

Depending on the family and the business, either model can work, although an office of the CEO is not as simple as having a single leader.

EXHIBIT 10

"Musts" For Co-CEOs

- Each successor-candidate is very capable, competent, and prepared for leadership.

- Candidates share fundamental goals, values, and levels of commitment.

- In addition to general leadership responsibilities, each potential co-successor has specific areas of responsibility.

- Candidates have solid relationships with one another. They demonstrate the ability to process and resolve differences constructively.

- An experienced board of directors, including respected outsiders, holds the CEO team accountable, gives perspective, and provides a safety net—for example, helping the family resolve disputes when it's at an impasse.

The family and especially the siblings as a group need to discuss what kind of leadership they want and what kind of leadership the business needs to take it forward. From such discussions, it will become clearer which of the siblings best fill the leadership needs of the family and the business and which leadership model is most likely to be successful.

It is important to keep in mind that the most dominant individuals or most charismatic personalities do not always make the best leaders. Challenges facing contemporary business leaders include constantly accelerating change, increased globalization, technological change, and shifts in the work force. **The leadership attributes required to meet these kinds of challenges, according to business owners and expert observers, include: a desire to serve the people you lead; self-awareness (enabling business owners to understand what kind of leadership style works best for them); ability to handle change, uncertainty, chaos, and ambiguity; having a vision of where the company is going; a clear set of values (because leadership grows out of the values the leader holds); openness, ranging from being a good student and listener to letting ideas percolate up; and trustworthiness.**

Because of the emotional intensity of a sibling partnership, **the trustworthiness of a leader is essential. Leaders earn trust when it is clear they are not out to dominate their brothers and sisters or tell them what to do. They are not "Bosses"—they are leaders.** A sibling should be able to say of the leader: "I'm comfortable with her and trust that she's making decisions that aren't going to harm me. I know she'll seek my support and my advice when It is appropriate and that she will know when It is appropriate and when it isn't. I'm confident that she will make decisions that benefit all of us and that she will

It should be apparent to the siblings that the leader's role is not just to hold them accountable but that the siblings, including the leader, will all hold each other accountable. A tremendous leadership skill is understanding when to act unilaterally, when a majority is required, and when total buy-in of the group is necessary.

50

do so in an impartial way and that she's willing to sacrifice her own personal gain for all of us. I'm sure she has all our best interests at heart." It should be apparent to the siblings that the leader's role is not just to hold them accountable but that the siblings, including the leader, will all hold each other accountable. A tremendous leadership skill is understanding when to act unilaterally, when a majority is required, and when total buy-in of the group is necessary.

To initiate the process of encouraging leadership to manifest itself, we recommend that members of the sibling team strengthen their understanding of each other and have open, honest discussions about their own and each other's strengths and weaknesses. They need to talk with each other about where the business is going and what its needs are, and to develop a common understanding about these issues. They can then examine how their strengths and weaknesses fit in with their vision of the business and begin to determine the roles they will take.

What generally happens is that, over time, someone surfaces as a coordinator, consensus builder or strategist. In short, leadership emerges. When it does, the emergence is so natural that, as we often have observed, one of the family members says, "You know what? Bob's acting as a leader." And other family members chime in: "You're right. He's the leader."

The process requires time. In families where sibling relationships are good, learning to work together and the emergence of leadership may take one to three years. In families where relationships are troubled, the process may take three or four years of hard work and involve a consulting professional who can help the siblings resolve difficult issues and relationships.

If a leader does not emerge naturally, then families may choose what appears to be a more deliberate process of selecting leadership, still keeping the decision with the siblings. One founder-parent with three children in the business and two outside proposed the following procedure for naming the next-generation business leader:

☛ Responsibility for choosing the successor would rest with the next generation since they would be the ones to live with the decision.

☛ The decision would have to be made in no more than 18 months. (Otherwise, the founder feared, the children would endlessly avoid making a choice.)

☛ How the decision was to be made was left to the siblings.

The siblings met several times to iron out a process. Here is what they agreed on:

☞ Siblings interested in being a candidate would submit, in writing, their qualifications for the job and their vision for the future. A family meeting would be devoted to asking questions of the candidates and hearing their answers.

☞ The siblings would decide the matter by voting. Each could vote for as many candidates as he or she wished. No candidate could be selected without at least two-thirds of the votes. If more than one candidate received that many votes, there would be a runoff (which, in this case, proved unnecessary).

☞ The votes would be tabulated by the two inactive siblings. All agreed that the results, other than who was elected, would never be known to the family members or to anyone else.

☞ Following the decision, everyone would agree that it was unanimous and support the selectee.

When asked if he felt he were the best qualified, the winner responded, "Yes and no." Psychological profiles assembled on each candidate suggested another sibling was better suited for the responsibilities of chief executive. But, he said, he felt he was selected because he had been devoted to family unity his entire life and he was able to present a cohesive vision for the future with everyone working together and using their particular strengths.

Here are some additional methods that families have used to resolve the issue of leadership of sibling teams:

- **When the best choice is clear, parents "bite the bullet" and appoint the next leader as early as possible.** If the ability of the first child to enter the business is exceptionally proven before his or her siblings get established, for example, it is usually best to make the decision and communicate it to the others. Making the selection early gives others time to adjust to the choice.

- The board of directors assists in the process. The outside nonfamily directors can provide an objective forum to address succession. They can:

  — help the family or the siblings define the most important capabilities of the next chief executive, based on the company's strategic needs.

— suggest job assignments that help successor candidates develop their strengths and compensate for their weaknesses.

— evaluate the siblings' performance.

— provide assurance that once the decision is made, the choice was fair and based on sound business judgment.

Whatever method is used, it is important for the family to rally around the new leader. His or her success depends on the support of the co-owning siblings and their commitment to the company's strategy. **This means the siblings must develop into a solid team—the company will be no stronger than the bond among its owners.**

Making Co-CEOs Effective

To answer the question of whether co-CEOs can work, just look at Nordstrom, the benchmark retailer, where six family members serve jointly as president. In the Nordstrom model, each person in the office of the president has responsibility for a key aspect of the business. Issues that affect the whole business are the purview of the joint presidency. The group meets regularly behind closed doors for honest and straightforward discussion. Disagreements are aired and discussions can be heated. Votes are taken. A key rule is that even if the vote is 4-2, the group leaves the room speaking with one voice.

Having co-CEOs may increase family unity, improve decision making, aid succession continuity, reduce family conflict, enhance authority, and strengthen communication. These are benefits that come from the synergy resulting from appropriately combining many people's strengths.

But problems like confused authority and slow decision making can result. Benefits can be achieved and detriments avoided if, before setting up an office of the CEO, several decisions are made and several rules are agreed upon.

☞ **Make Important Decisions Together and Speak with One Voice.** Following the Nordstrom example, members of the office of CEO must present themselves as a single, unified voice. The notion of "I" should be erased and the idea of "we, the CEO" must be emphasized.

When employees see members of an office of CEO having diverse opinions, they will become confused as to whom to follow and may play the old game of "going to the right person" to get the

53

right answer. Just like an individual CEO who lets his top team know his mind is not made up, a CEO team in disagreement will be lobbied extensively.

Such lobbying creates coalitions that interfere with team unity. Indeed, it is a vicious cycle where the more disagreement the team exhibits, the more its members will be lobbied, furthering disagreement and causing even greater lobbying.

While CEO team members can argue in private, they must never argue publicly. Arguments, particularly about important decisions, can make shareholders, employees, and others feel insecure.

☛ **Decide first what decisions will be group decisions and how group decisions will be made.** We strongly recommend CEO groups use simple majority voting on all but the most important decisions. This decreases the time needed to make decisions and helps keep arguments from becoming too personal. Certain decisions, like major acquisitions or divestitures, may require a super majority or even unanimity.

☛ **Support all decisions made by individual CEO team members.** Of course, making decisions together all the time is impossible. Every team member should have distinct, specific, and agreed-to areas of responsibility and defined levels of authority and autonomy.

Areas of responsibility would mean all parts of the company with a measurable bottom line or key staff areas like finance and accounting, human resources, sales and marketing, production and operations. Levels of authority and autonomy refer to how big a decision has to be before it must be brought to the entire CEO team. Usually, a dollar amount is determined as a guide.

Other issues that may need to be brought to the whole team are personnel moves of senior executives, discussions with the press or any other activity that may influence the company's external image, and any activity involving shareholders or members of the board of directors.

☛ Other basic decisions include criteria for inclusion on the CEO team, who should be on the team, and how people might be removed from the team. A meeting secretary and a meeting chair should be chosen, with a term of office defined for each. A meeting schedule should be arranged, with meetings no less frequent than weekly. Rules for calling special meetings should be spelled out.

While we find that having more than one CEO is possible, we do not recommend this structure for all — or even most — family businesses. If a family firm is blessed with multiple talented and compatible leaders, choosing one above others could be destructive to family and business. But we also see too many situations where *failing* to choose one leader among several candidates paralyzes a company. Faced with several highly capable successors, too many parent/CEOs feel forced to make a choice. Faced with a clear choice of one successor, too many parent/CEOs feel more comfortable with multi-leader scenarios.

Either way—having a single CEO or an office of the CEO—can work if the circumstances are right. If the conditions in which the right choice can be made and implemented aren't developed, either way can lead to disaster for the business and the family.

IX. *Communication Between Team and Parents*

In a printing company we'll call Hubbard Graphics, Dad learned that his three kids were considering purchasing a very expensive German press. Yes, he knew he had put them in charge and begun semi-retirement. But he thought buying the press would be a big mistake. It was just too costly and the company was not doing the kind of printing that would require such a machine. Dad scoffed at the kids' argument that a press like this would boost Hubbard Graphics beyond its competitors and enable it to take on many kinds of jobs it had been incapable of doing before. He was sure that before they knew it, they would be in debt way over their heads and the contracts they envisioned just wouldn't materialize.

Dad thought he knew how he could head off catastrophe. He convinced Mom to try to talk their daughter, Ellen, out of the idea— Mom and Ellen had an especially good relationship, and Dad was sure Mom could persuade Ellen that the purchase was a bad idea. Dad himself would collar Steve, the younger son; they usually saw eye-to-eye. And if Dad could convince Steve and Mom could convince Ellen, then Rob, the older son, would have to give in.

What a surprise when Dad poked his head in Steve's office. Steve welcomed him warmly and listened attentively for a few minutes while his father tried to persuade him of the foolishness of buying the press. "Dad," he said, "it makes me uncomfortable to have you speaking to me about this privately. Rob and Ellen and I are committed to working as a team. Why don't you come and talk to all three of us at our executive committee meeting next week? We'll put you on the agenda. We want to hear your views and eventually we'll make a decision. But it will be a team decision." And, as Mom reported to Dad, she had a similar result during her visit with Ellen.

As long as parents want to be in the information loop and use information constructively, the sibling team should usually keep them up to date on what's going on in the business even if Mom and Dad are no longer owners. This doesn't mean, however, that parents be permitted to interfere inappropriately with the team's decisions. In the scenario above, Dad Hubbard clearly thinks he can divide and conquer by trading on individual relationships and lobbying the children. But the children know their father. Long ago, when they were in the early stages of their partnership, they worked out how they would respond if Dad disagreed with their business decisions and ideas: As a unit.

When siblings form a partnership, they are faced with the question not only of how they will communicate with each other but also how they will communicate with their parents, with nonfamily employees, and with the outside world (in some businesses, for example, a particular sibling is assigned the responsibility of speaking with the media).

Even if they have given up all their stock, parents may still want to be involved and included. In a sense, the parents have a permanent right to be members of the "joint venture" with their children, unless they clearly exclude themselves—"You really don't have to talk to us about what your agenda is before you have your meetings. We trust you completely and, besides, we're too busy." Until parents give that signal, the sibling team needs to keep them appropriately informed.

Siblings may find that, like some parents, some nonfamily executives may try to divide and conquer. And like some parents, nonfamily executives may also "triangulate"—complaining about one sibling to another.

We suggest that siblings develop some rules about how the team will communicate with those outside the team and make this a part of the code of conduct.

EXHIBIT 11 ▐███████████████████████████████▌

Eight Steps to Better Communication

1. Listen well. Make sure you understand the meaning behind the words.

2. Seek understanding, not victory.

3. Don't let disagreements fester.

4. Disagree without being disagreeable.

5. Create a "safe" environment for discussion. Don't judge. Accept your siblings' right to their own feelings and conclusions.

6. Complain directly, not through a third party.

7. Put the past behind you. Don't assume that your adult siblings are the same people they were as children.

8. Avoid certainty. Conclusive statements—"That will never work!"—shut off discussion.

X. *Remember, It's a Family*

With the members of your sibling team spending so much time in the business and so much time with each other, you may lose sight of what family business is all about: Family. That is, each sibling's own nuclear family and extended family—Mom and Dad, brothers and sisters and their spouses, and your nieces and nephews. Without their love, happiness, good will and support, a sibling partnership can falter.

The best advice? Have fun together. Spend time with your own spouse and children, of course. But you and your family should also spend time socially with your siblings and their families.

You may feel that you already spend so much time with your siblings at work that you don't want to spend even more time with them away from the business. But this kind of social time serves a special purpose: it enables your spouse and children and their spouses and children to see that all is well among you and your siblings. It also helps them better understand one another so that they will want to support the continuation of the family business.

Some ideas: Go on family retreats together. Work together on a family philanthropy project. Go on outings as a group—a picnic in the park or a day at the beach.

Look for ways to have the children—the cousins—spend time together as tots and toddlers and preschoolers. An important goal is to create good memories for the children as a family, because that contributes to the effort to have the business continue across generations. When you create an environment in which cousins have a good time together as small children, you're taking some of the first steps to position them for success as the next generation of cousin owners and leaders of the family business.

Be sure to include siblings who are not working in the business. When the business moves to the third generation, it will enter a period when more family members will not be active in the business. But they still need to be included as full members of the family, and how you include nonactive family members now will create a model for the future.

XI. *Preparing for the Next (Cousin) Generation*

Two brothers, Andrew and John Woods, inherited their parents' business 50-50. For many years, times were good, Woods Electronics did well, and the brothers got along. But Andrew, the older of the two and president of the company, overlooked it when John borrowed money from the company and didn't pay it back. John had a big family to support, after all. And in Andrew's view, John didn't work very hard or take on his share of the responsibility, even though their salaries were equal. However, Andrew got to run the company the way he wanted to and John didn't interfere.

Then business turned sour, and the brothers began to fight over the company's strategic direction. For three years, they battled each other, with one trying to wrest control from the other. They even ended up in court. The once-thriving company with more than 250 employees shrunk to less than 60 workers. Finally, Andrew sold his half of the business to John and got out. The brothers have not spoken to each other since and their families have nothing to do with one another.

Andrew is exceptionally bitter. For him, the family business is gone. He can't pass it on to his sons and daughters.

He blames his parents for passing the business along in equal shares instead of giving controlling interest to one brother or the other, preferably himself. But even if he had received 51 percent and his brother had received 49 percent, the story would probably still not have had a happy ending. No structure had ever been created to support a partnership. The company had no board of directors. The brothers had no code of conduct, no buy-sell agreement, no formal strategic planning process. The more Andrew and John disagreed with each other, the more their wives took sides, causing their relationship to deteriorate even further. And Andrew did not treat his brother like an adult, nor did he hold John accountable for his behavior.

In contrast, two other brothers, Rick and Larry Robertson, inherited Robertson Metals, the business their father started. They, fortunately, had grown up learning to respect each other and to work together as equals. Jointly, they made a commitment to do what was best for the business. Nearly 20 years ago, they hired a nonfamily vice president, Michael, whom family members today describe as "brilliant."

61

Michael not only helped Rick and Larry begin to professionalize the company but he also impressed on them the need to look down the road and think about the long-range future of the company and the family. He encouraged them to do estate and succession planning and, despite their initial fears about bringing family into the business, to start inviting members of the third generation to join the company.

Today, half a dozen of the Robertson cousins—all of whom have solid experience outside the company—work in the business. Encouraged by their fathers and guided by Michael, they assumed responsibility for building the company even further. They volunteered to take on the task of succession planning and recently, the cousins elected Larry's daughter, Georgia, as president and CEO of the company, and Rick's son, Richard, as executive vice president. Larry passed away several years ago, but Rick continues as chairman of the company.

The cousins have created a new governing structure for the company consisting of four groups:

(1) A management committee that includes Georgia, Richard, and four key nonfamily executives; it meets weekly and oversees day-to-day operations.

(2) An internal owners group made up of the third-generation cousins and siblings who work in the company. It addresses broader issues that can't be resolved by the management committee.

(3) An expanded owners committee that includes cousins and siblings both inside and outside the company as well as spouses. A great vehicle for communication about the business, it meets twice a year to share financial statements and other information.

(4) An advisory board made up of selected family members, key nonfamily executives, and three outside business leaders.

What was a very small company when Rick and Larry inherited it grew significantly under their leadership and is growing still. It now does well over $100 million in annual sales and employs more than 700 people. And the cousins are already consciously preparing for the fourth generation of family leadership and ownership.

Why has the Robertson family been so successful in preserving the business for the family? For one thing, family members placed great value on family harmony and their commitment to each other. Rick and Larry encouraged their children to attend family business seminars, where they gained skills and knowledge that they brought back to the business and the family.

The cousins say that Michael served as an excellent mentor. But the real key was the superb example their fathers set for them. "The one thread that wove its way through our thinking was the marvelous relationship that Larry and Rick had as a team," says Georgia. In their meetings, she continues, the cousins would often reflect on the spirit of family that their fathers represented to them and they committed themselves to emulating that spirit.

These two stories — of the Woods brothers and of the Robertson family — underscore the critical importance of the sibling generation. What happens at the sibling stage will influence forever what happens in the business and in the family. Will both family and business crumble, as they did in the Woods family? Or, as they are now doing in the Robertson family, will the business and family thrive and look forward to yet another generation because of the loving team spirit exemplified by siblings in the second generation?

XII. *Summary*

A successful sibling partnership requires enormous dedication and hard work on the part of parents, spouses, and—most especially—the siblings themselves.

Parents can help by treating the siblings as a unit, giving them challenging tasks to work on as a team, and resisting the temptation to intervene when things don't go smoothly.

Husbands and wives support the team by educating themselves about the business and about family business in general. They'll find it wise to get to know all the family members directly instead of through the filter of their spouses' views. Instead of taking sides with their spouses over family grievances, husbands and wives can help keep relationships on track by asking good questions and getting their spouses to look at issues from several sides.

If you are in the sibling group, you will enhance your chances for success if you commit yourselves to being a unit and take the steps necessary to gain skills in communication, conflict resolution, and shared decision making. Your chances will be further strengthened by creating an infrastructure of governance, policies, and procedures that provides the framework for effective planning and decision making and for accountability. Such an infrastructure also supports harmony in the team by making decisions less personal and more professional, and by encouraging all team members to perform at their highest level and conduct themselves in a mature fashion. The infrastructure includes having a board of directors with respected, independent outsiders on it, and holding a variety of business and family meetings that enhance communication and decision making.

As a sibling team, you will find that you have to be vigilant and sensitive to what is going on around you. You will need to be sure that actions by Mom and Dad are not divisive to the group. You will need to take action to make sure that all spouses are made to feel part of the sibling partnership, so that you will have their support. You need to make sure that you all speak with one voice to nonfamily employees, giving them the respect due them but not letting them play one of you against the other.

You need to nurture your personal relationships with one another. Having fun, enjoying one another's company, and finding shared interests outside the business will help you weather rough patches inside the business.

And finally, emphasizing your common ground and focusing on a goal larger than yourselves will go a long way toward holding you together as a team and enabling you to deal with your individual differences.

Sibling partnerships are an increasingly common phenomenon. As you build your team, keep in mind that the sibling stage presents some of the greatest challenges—and opportunities—that a family business can face. Take heart from the success of other sibling partnerships and pledge yourselves to be a positive model for those yet to come.

Index

67

69

The Authors

Craig E. Aronoff and John L. Ward have long been recognized as leaders in the family business field. Founding principals of **The Family Business Consulting Group**, they work with hundreds of family businesses around the world. Recipients of the Family Firm Institute's Beckhard Award for outstanding contributions to family business practice, they have spoken to family business audiences on every continent. Their books include *Family Business Sourcebook II*, and the three-volume series *The Future of Private Enterprise*.

Craig E. Aronoff, Ph.D., holds the Dinos Distinguished Chair of Private Enterprise and is professor of management at Kennesaw State University (Atlanta). He founded and directs the university's Family Enterprise Center. The center focuses on education and research for family businesses, and its programs have been emulated by more than 100 universities worldwide. In addition to his undergraduate degree from Northwestern University and Masters from the University of Pennsylvania, he holds a Ph.D. in organizational communication from the University of Texas.

John L. Ward, Ph.D., is the Ralph Marotta Professor of Private Enterprise at Loyola University Chicago. He teaches strategic management and business leadership at Loyola's Graduate School of Business, and is a regular visiting lecturer at two European business schools. He has previously been dean of undergraduate business at Loyola and a senior associate with Strategic Planning Institute (PIMS Program) in Cambridge, Massachusetts. A graduate of Northwestern University (B.A.) and Stanford Graduate School of Business (M.B.A. and Ph.D.), his *Keeping the Family Business Healthy* and *Creating Effective Boards for Private Enterprises* are leading books in the family business field.

Joseph H. Astrachan, Ph.D., a principal of **The Family Business Consulting Group**, is the Wachovia Chair of Family Business, associate director and research director of the Family Enterprise Center at Kennesaw State University. He received a lifetime achievement award for his research on family business from the International Family Business Program Association. Astrachan is editor of *Family Business Review*, a scholarly publication of the Family Firm Institute.

Drew S. Mendoza, a principal and president of **The Family Business Consulting Group**, was founding director of the Loyola University Chicago Family Business Center, which is recognized as a leading think tank on issues unique to business-owning families. He is a member of the Family Firm Institute's board and an associate editor of the *Family Business Review.* Mendoza specializes in working with sibling and cousin owner/management teams, and with large shareholder groups in family businesses. A popular speaker, Mendoza has made numerous presentations to family business audiences and professional associations.

NEW PRICES EFFECTIVE OCTOBER 1, 1999

Order Form
Prepayment is required

Please Send Me:

_____ copies, #1 *Family Business Succession: The Final Test of Greatness*
_____ copies, #2 *Family Meetings: How to Build a Stronger Family and a Stronger Business*
_____ copies, #3 *Another Kind of Hero: Preparing Successors for Leadership*
_____ copies, #4 *How Families Work Together*
_____ copies, #5 *Family Business Compensation*
_____ copies, #6 *How to Choose & Use Advisors: Getting the Best Professional Family Business Advice*
_____ copies, #7 *Financing Transitions: Managing Capital and Liquidity in the Family Business*
_____ copies, #8 *Family Business Governance: Maximizing Family and Business Potential*
_____ copies, #9 *Preparing Your Family Business for Strategic Change*
_____ copies, #10 *Making Sibling Teams Work: The Next Generation*
_____ copies, #11 *Developing Family Business Policies: Your Guide to the Future*
_____ copies, #12 *Family Business Values: How to Assure a Legacy of Continuity & Success*
_____ copies, #13 *More Than Family: Non-Family Executives in the Family Business*
$_____ **Leadership Series Cost** (number of books x price – See chart below)
_____ *Keeping the Family Business Healthy* $24.95 X _____ copies
_____ *Creating Effective Boards For Private Enterprises* $39.95 X _____ copies
_____ *Family Business Sourcebook II* $69.00 X _____ copies
$_____ **Subtotal**
_____ Add 7% (Foreign 10% for Surface mail) Shipping to <u>Subtotal</u>
_____ *The Family Business ADVISOR* Monthly newsletter -- *$149* yearly*
$_____ **Total**
$_____ **GA residents add 5% sales tax to** <u>Total</u>
$_____ **Grand Total** (US dollars only)

*Add $15 U.S. Currency – Canada and Mexico / $30 U.S. Currency – All other Countries

Please charge my: MC _____ Visa _____ Amex _____   Check Enclosed _____

Account No. _____ Exp._____

Signature_____

SHIP TO:

Name_____

Company_____

Address_____

City _____ State _____ Zip_____

Country_____

Tel (_____)_____

E-mail _____

Leadership Series Multi-Volume Discounts *(any title combination)*	
1 – 9 books:	$16.95 ea.
10-24 books:	$14.95 ea.
25-49 books:	$12.50 ea.
50-99 books:	$ 10.00 ea.
100+ books:	$ 8.50 ea.

MAIL TO:

Business Owner Resources
1220-B Kennestone Circle
PO Box 4356
Marietta, GA 30061-4356
E-mail: fbop@family-business.net
Website: www.fbop.com
Fax: 770-425-1776
Tel: 800-551-0633/770-425-6673